Pavel Durov and the Celebrities Secrets Saga

Exploring the Complex Intersection of Privacy,
Criminal Activity, and the Quest for Online Safety
in the Age of Digital Communication

Helen Alems

Copyright © 2024 by Helen Alems

All rights reserved. No part of this publication may be reproduced, distributed, or transmitted in any form or by any means, including photocopying, recording, or other electronic or mechanical methods, without the prior written permission of the publisher, except in the case of brief quotations embodied in critical reviews and certain other noncommercial uses permitted by copyright law

Table of Contents

Introduction..5
    The Emergence of Telegram: A Synopsis............................. 5
    Digital Communication's Dual Nature............................8

Chapter 1: The Allure of Telegram..11
    Features that Draw People in...11
    The Security and Privacy Appeal...13
    The Telegram User Base: Who Uses It and Why?................. 16

Chapter 2: Criminal Underbelly: The Dark Side of Telegram.. 20
    Case Studies Concerning Criminal Behavior........................ 20
    The Significance of Anonymity in Illegal Exchanges............ 22
    Radicalization and Extremism: A Hateful Platform............23

Chapter 3: Legal and Ethical Implications.......................... 26
    Public Safety vs. Privacy: The Continual Debate..................26
    Difficulties for Law Enforcement in the Digital Age............ 28
    The Laws Governing Messaging Applications......................30

Chapter 4: Telegram's Response to Controversy................ 34
    Policy and Terms of Service Changes.....................................34
    The Significance of Pavel Durov's Detention........................ 36
    Actions Taken to Stop Illegal Behavior on the Platform...... 38

Chapter 5: The Future of Messaging Apps......................... 42
    Changing Privacy Concerns and User Expectations............42
    Balancing Safety and Freedom of Speech............................. 44

Suggestions for Communicating in a Changing Environment 47

Conclusion... 50

Thoughts on the Difficult Character of Communication... 50

The Way Ahead: Handling Security and Privacy in the Digital Age.. 52

Introduction

The Emergence of Telegram: A Synopsis

Since its 2013 inception, Telegram has been a prominent participant in the digital communication landscape, having been founded by Pavel Durov, the man behind Russia's largest social network, VKontakte (VK). Offering features like end-to-end encryption, self-destructing messages, and extensive cloud storage, Telegram set itself apart with its dedication to privacy, fulfilling its objective to deliver a safe and easy-to-use messaging network. By 2024, the app will have over 950 million active users, demonstrating its rapid growth in popularity.

Numerous important reasons have contributed to the platform's growth. First, people who are leery of corporate data mining and government spying have found resonance with its significant emphasis on user privacy. With users looking for a safer alternative to popular messaging apps like Facebook Messenger or WhatsApp, Telegram's guarantee of anonymity emerged as a light in a world growing more and more alarmed about data breaches and privacy violations. However, the app's emphasis on secrecy has also drawn users with bad intents, such as members of extremist and criminal organizations.

The adaptability of Telegram has also contributed to its growth. In contrast to many messaging apps that are just concerned with personal communication, Telegram has a large feature set to meet the needs of a variety of users. Large group chats, channels for message broadcasting to an infinite number of viewers, and a variety of bots that improve user experience are also supported. Thanks to these capabilities, Telegram is now more than simply a chat app—it's a platform for marketing, community interaction, and information sharing.

Telegram's allure is international, as seen by its considerable rise in popularity in a number of nations, especially those with strict internet regulations. Telegram has become an indispensable communication tool for journalists, activists, and regular people looking to organize, disseminate information, and voice dissent in areas where traditional social media is prohibited. Its ability to provide anonymous communication has given it a double-edged effect, encouraging both criminal activity and beneficial social initiatives.

This dualism has not gone ignored, though. Telegram is under investigation by governments and law enforcement organizations all over the world as it grows. The platform has come under fire for what is seen as its inability to control illicit activity and its part in encouraging crime. As we examine the intricacies of Telegram, this conflict between its dedication to privacy and the demand for responsibility will be a major subject.

Digital Communication's Dual Nature

Digital communication has completely changed how people communicate, connect, and share information with one other. Although this change has made people more powerful and connected, it has also brought up new difficulties and complications that may be abused or misused. With messaging apps like Telegram, the dual character of digital communication—its capacity to both increase individual freedom and enable criminal activity—becomes more clear.

Digital communication channels have brought about the democratization of information exchange. Users can engage in conversations that cut over geographic borders, interact with people all around the world, and share ideas. As a result, thriving online communities have emerged where people can mobilize for social causes, share experiences, and find support. For instance, during social

Chapter 1: The Allure of Telegram

Features that Draw People in

Telegram distinguishes itself in a competitive messaging app market with its special features that improve user experience and encourage community participation. The feature that lets it accommodate big group chats and channels is one of its most pleasant features. Up to 200,000 people can join groups that users can create, facilitating in-depth conversations and teamwork among friends, family, and interest-based communities. Conversely, channels have the ability to broadcast messages to an infinite number of subscribers, which makes them the perfect platform for influencers, news organizations, and content creators looking to reach a larger audience.

Telegram's bot capabilities is another noteworthy feature that draws people in. Bots are automated programs that can do a lot of different things, such playing games and filling out surveys, to arranging events and giving news updates. Because of these bots' adaptability, developers have created thousands of bots to meet a variety of interests and requirements. By customizing their Telegram experience, users can interact with the app in ways that are frequently not feasible on other platforms.

Users can transmit voice messages, documents, movies, images, and text messages using the platform's rich media sharing features. Large documents and media can be easily shared among users without depending on third-party file-sharing services, thanks to the ability to distribute files up to 2 GB in size. The software also allows for creative expression and improves communication with features like GIFs, stickers, and customized themes.

Telegram's emphasis on dependability and quickness is another characteristic that makes it unique. The application is meant to work flawlessly even in situations with poor connectivity because it is based on a decentralized infrastructure. Because of its dependability, Telegram is especially useful in areas with erratic internet connectivity because it keeps users connected no matter what.

Finally, the software offers a great deal of power and customization to users. To better organize their chats, users can create folders, change chat backdrops, and modify their notification settings. Because of its high degree of personalization, Telegram is more than simply a messaging app—it's a flexible tool for communication. Users may customize their experience to suit their preferences.

The Security and Privacy Appeal

Telegram's strong privacy and security policies are among its biggest selling points; these are aspects that are highly relevant in the current digital environment. As consumers become more concerned about data breaches, monitoring, and improper use of personal information, they are looking for platforms that put security first. Telegram appeals to people who are concerned about their privacy because it takes several steps to address these issues.

With its Secret Chats, Telegram uses end-to-end encryption to make sure that only the sender and the recipient can see the messages. Users can feel secure and private knowing that not even Telegram can access the content of these discussions thanks to encryption. To give users even more control over their data, the app also has capabilities like self-destructing messages that erase themselves automatically after a predetermined amount of time.

Furthermore, Telegram is dedicated to protecting user privacy in ways other than chatting. In order to register an account on the platform, users are not need to submit personal information like a phone number. The anonymity is especially useful for people who want to interact without disclosing who they are. In order to facilitate communication without revealing personal information, the software also provides users with the option to communicate with others using usernames rather than phone numbers.

Telegram's attractiveness is increased by its openness regarding its data policies. The platform routinely releases transparency reports that include all of the requests it gets from law enforcement and governmental bodies. Users are reassured by this dedication to transparency that their data is not being exploited or sold to outside parties.

Telegram distinguishes out as a platform that places a high priority on privacy in a world where many well-known apps face backlash for how they handle user data. Because of its well-established image as a secure place where people can express themselves without worrying about censorship or surveillance, activists, journalists, and regular users find the app to be appealing.

The Telegram User Base: Who Uses It and Why?

Users on Telegram come from a variety of backgrounds and have a wide range of interests. The software is appealing to a wide range of people, including tech-savvy people, privacy enthusiasts, social activists, and even companies. Understanding who uses Telegram and why can help one understand why it's becoming more and more popular.

A sizable portion of Telegram's user base is made up of those looking for more privacy. Users tend to gravitate toward platforms that stress security in an era where privacy infractions and data breaches are common. People who are worried about monitoring are drawn to Telegram because of its reputation for protecting user data, especially in areas with repressive governments or restrictions on free speech. Telegram is a popular tool used by journalists and activists to coordinate movements, exchange information, and communicate safely without worrying about government intervention.

Younger users are another important group, as they are lured to Telegram's cutting-edge capabilities and engaging user interface. This group finds value in the platform's capacity to have big group conversations and channels, which enables them to discuss their interests, pastimes, and social causes. People who like to express themselves creatively and engage in interactive dialogue find Telegram to be the preferred platform due to the inclusion of bots and multimedia sharing, which improves their communication experience.

A sizable segment of Telegram's user base consists of companies and content producers. Through channels and bots, the platform offers marketers an efficient way to engage with their audience. Businesses utilize Telegram to build a sense of community among their followers by sharing promotions, updates, and insightful material. Because of the app's intuitive features, businesses can interact directly with their audience and offer individualized communication, something that standard social media platforms frequently fail to deliver.

Moreover, Telegram's popularity is not limited by geography. In areas where other messaging apps are restricted or censored, it has become incredibly popular. Telegram is an essential communication tool for anyone looking for a platform free from government control in nations like Russia, China, and Iran.

Telegram's distinctive features, dedication to privacy, and wide user base contribute to its appeal. Telegram continues to draw in a diverse range of people and businesses as users look for platforms that offer security and innovation, securing its place as a major participant in the messaging industry.

Chapter 2: Criminal Underbelly: The Dark Side of Telegram

Case Studies Concerning Criminal Behavior

Once praised for its robust encryption and respect for user privacy, the messaging service Telegram has also turned into a haven for criminal activity. Although the software has a lot to offer law-abiding users, those involved in illicit activities have been drawn to it because of its emphasis on security and anonymity. A range of illegal activities, from drug trafficking to hacking services, are shown by case studies of criminal use on Telegram. These activities are frequently coordinated using private channels and closed groups.

One well-known instance is the growth of black marketplaces for drugs. After significant darknet marketplaces like Silk Road and AlphaBay were shut down, a lot of drug sellers and buyers resorted to Telegram to carry on their business. Under law enforcement's radar, users may plan drug delivery, send and receive secure messages, and accept cryptocurrency payments through closed groups on the app. In an Italian case from 2020, law enforcement took action against a drug trafficking organization whose members concealed their identities behind encrypted messages and pseudonyms. This particular case highlighted the possibility of the platform aiding in the drug trade.

Cybercrime is a big additional area. Telegram is used by hackers and thieves to distribute malware, sell stolen data, and provide hacking services. Cybersecurity experts discovered multiple Telegram groups in 2021 that were used to exchange credit card numbers, credit hack credentials, and even private medical information. These illicit transactions occur in comparatively closed communities that are protected by the security features of the app and the platform's lax control.

The Significance of Anonymity in Illegal Exchanges

Because of its steadfast dedication to user privacy and anonymity, Telegram is particularly appealing to illicit behavior. In contrast to other social networking sites that demand real-name verification or retain a lot of user data, Telegram lets users register accounts with very little data—often simply a phone number. The emphasis on anonymity makes it very difficult to identify the people behind illicit transactions, which allows criminals to operate with a certain amount of impunity.

Telegram enables private conversations with end-to-end encryption and messages that self-destruct in addition to privacy. Illegal transactions routinely take advantage of this functionality. It is nearly hard for law authorities to track down communications or obtain evidence when these covert discussions are used to arrange the sale of fake goods, traffic guns, or even engage in human trafficking. Burner phones or temporary numbers are frequently used by illegal vendors to open Telegram accounts, keeping their identities secret even in the case that law enforcement spies on them.

The anonymity Telegram offers makes it easier for people to use cryptocurrency in shady transactions. Because cryptocurrencies like Bitcoin allow for some degree of untraceability, many criminals want to utilize them for payments. When paired with encrypted communications, this forms an almost perfect system for executing illicit transactions without being discovered.

Radicalization and Extremism: A Hateful Platform

Extremist movements and groups have also been drawn to Telegram because of its emphasis on privacy and encryption capabilities. The platform has developed into a focal point for propaganda, hate speech, and recruiting by far-right, Islamist, and other extremist organizations in recent years. Telegram is the perfect medium for these groups to disseminate their beliefs and draw in new members because it allows for the hosting of private channels and massive group chats.

The use of Telegram by ISIS sympathizers and recruiters is one prominent example. The gang has recruited people all across the world, shared propaganda movies, and distributed attack planning manuals over the network. These groups have not been discouraged by Telegram's quick removal of extremist information from its public spaces; instead, they have moved to hidden conversations and private channels, which make their operations more clandestine and challenging to police. Similar patterns have been seen in far-right extremist groups in Western nations, where demands for violence, xenophobia, and racism are frequently promoted via Telegram.

This problem has become worse due to the platform's inadequate moderating of private channels. Despite Telegram's efforts to combat extremism, including the banning of public groups associated with terrorism, many groups persist in their more covert operations. Telegram's secrecy and encryption make it a safe refuge for those hoping to incite hatred, radicalize others, and plot violent acts without drawing attention from law enforcement.

Despite the fact that Telegram's dedication to security and privacy benefits a large number of users, it has also made it a desirable venue for extremism and criminal activities. Concerns have been raised concerning its participation in the shadowy areas of the internet due to its facilitation of unlawful transactions, cybercrime, and the promotion of extremist beliefs through its encrypted chats, private groups, and anonymity capabilities.

Chapter 3: Legal and Ethical Implications

Public Safety vs. Privacy: The Continual Debate

With the popularity of encrypted messaging services like Telegram, the argument between privacy and public safety has become more heated. On the one hand, proponents of privacy contend that people ought to be allowed to interact without worrying about being watched by the government or harmed by businesses. This is particularly crucial in nations with authoritarian governments, as encrypted platforms provide a lifeline for individuals, journalists, and activists who want to express themselves freely without worrying about retaliation. However, governments and law enforcement organizations contend that anonymous communications and robust encryption might cover terrorists, criminals, and other undesirable actors, making it more difficult to ensure public safety.

Telegram is at the center of this discussion because of its emphasis on privacy with features like end-to-end encryption, private chats, and less data retention. These features shield users from unauthorized monitoring, but they also give people who want to commit crimes a place to do so without worrying about getting caught. For example, terrorist groups use Telegram as a forum for radicalization and propaganda, while criminal organizations utilize it to traffic in drugs, weapons, and even people.

Increased regulation of encrypted messaging apps has been called for due to the conflict between privacy and public safety. For the interest of public safety, governments contend that tech corporations ought to open backdoors or grant law enforcement some access. Privacy activists respond that if encryption were to degrade, hackers and other bad actors as well as law enforcement might exploit backdoors, jeopardizing everyone's security. There is still disagreement between the parties over how much privacy can be protected without jeopardizing public safety, so the argument has not ended.

Difficulties for Law Enforcement in the Digital Age

Using encrypted messaging apps like Telegram presents substantial hurdles for law enforcement organizations worldwide. By ensuring that only the intended recipients of a message can see its contents, end-to-end encryption negates the effectiveness of traditional investigative techniques like eavesdropping or communication monitoring. Telegram asserts that it does not save the private encryption keys, so even if law enforcement intercepts the conversation, they will be unable to decode it.

Due to this, law enforcement is facing an increasing number of "going dark" situations in which they are unable to obtain information that is necessary for conducting investigations into acts of terrorism, organized crime, and other criminal activity. Telegram's anonymity adds to the complexity by allowing users to register for accounts without disclosing their genuine names, which makes it challenging to find and follow suspects. International investigations are further complicated by the fact that Telegram's servers are frequently situated in nations with lax or inconsistent data preservation laws.

Law enforcement has used a mix of digital forensic methods, group infiltration, and member emulation to obtain information in order to overcome these obstacles. In certain instances, authorities have created intricate techniques to take advantage of weaknesses in suspects' gadgets in order to get beyond encryption. The encryption arms race goes on despite these efforts, with messaging apps enhancing their privacy features in response to ethical and legal concerns. In light of encryption, law enforcement is forced to consider how to adjust to a reality in which conventional surveillance instruments are becoming less and less useful.

The Laws Governing Messaging Applications

varied legal systems around the world have varied laws governing encrypted messaging apps like Telegram. These differences are a reflection of cultural views on privacy, government control, and the place of technology in society. Apps must abide by rules like the General Data Protection Regulation (GDPR) in nations with strict data protection laws, like those in the European Union. GDPR requires messaging services to safeguard user data and guarantee openness about the gathering, use, and storage of personal data. GDPR does not, however, require businesses to offer backdoors to encrypted communications, which irritates governments when trying to obtain data for criminal investigations.

The Communications Assistance for Law Enforcement Act (CALEA), which mandates telecom firms to support law enforcement in intercepting communications, shapes the legal environment in the United States. Over-the-top (OTT) services like Telegram are exempt from CALEA, therefore unlike regular phone carriers, the app is not required to abide by wiretapping demands. Discussions over whether new laws should be passed to force messaging providers to cooperate with criminal investigations while protecting user privacy rights have arisen as a result of this legal loophole.

Other nations approach encrypted messaging apps with greater vigor. For instance, Telegram was temporarily prohibited in Russia because the company refused to provide the government access to encryption keys, despite the government's desire to read user messages for security reasons. Despite Telegram's opposition, a settlement was finally struck and the restriction was lifted; however, the specifics of that arrangement are still unknown. Similar restrictions apply to messaging apps in nations like China and Iran, where certain platforms are completely barred for defying requests from the government for increased surveillance.

Governments everywhere are having difficulty coming up with a unified legal system that strikes a balance between the interests of law enforcement, national security, and privacy. While some nations have focused on promoting international collaboration to combat cross-border illicit activities, others have advocated legislation requiring platforms to incorporate backdoors or face penalties. In the end, as technology develops, the legal environment around messaging apps is probably going to change, and finding a balance between security and privacy is still a hot button topic.

Chapter 4: Telegram's Response to Controversy

Policy and Terms of Service Changes

The debates regarding Telegram's involvement in supporting unlawful activity, disseminating extremist information, and acting as a medium for illicit transactions intensified along with the app's rise in popularity. Over the years, Telegram has made multiple modifications to its policies and terms of service (ToS) in response to increasing criticism from governments and advocacy groups. The improvements were intended to achieve a compromise between addressing concerns regarding the platform's potential for criminal use and upholding user privacy, which has long been a core feature.

The public position that Telegram took against extremism and unlawful content was one significant shift. The app has taken steps to censor content in public channels and groups, even if it still maintains a policy of not actively monitoring private talks. These days, Telegram's rules of service expressly prohibit encouraging acts of terrorism, violence, or illicit activity like selling guns or smuggling drugs. When it comes to blocking and eliminating public channels that break these guidelines, the firm has been more aggressive. For instance, hate speech and propaganda linked to ISIS have been targeted and shut down, despite the fact that these groups frequently reappear under various identities.

A noteworthy addition to Telegram's policy is the inclusion of reporting methods. Telegram added capabilities that enable users to report content related to child abuse, terrorism, and other criminal acts in response to concerns expressed by law enforcement and human rights organizations. The platform moderators examine these reports, and if necessary, they block or report violating accounts or channels to the relevant authorities. Despite these initiatives, Telegram has come under fire for not going far enough to stop illicit activity because a huge number of these transactions occur in secret chats or private channels that are encrypted and generally inaccessible.

The Significance of Pavel Durov's Detention

Co-founder and CEO of Telegram Pavel Durov is renowned for his unwavering support of free speech and privacy, even in the face of criticism from the government. The 2014 Russian detention of Durov had a significant effect on Telegram's development as well as Durov's personal life path. The Russian authorities put pressure on Durov, who was in charge of VKontakte, the biggest social network in Russia, to give up user information belonging to opposition activists. His refusal resulted in his expulsion from VKontakte and ultimate banishment from Russia. Durov's approach to Telegram was strongly impacted by his experience with state overreach, which reinforced his conviction that user privacy and resistance to censorship are crucial.

Tensions between Telegram and other countries around the world also increased as a result of Durov's imprisonment. Specifically, Telegram has been at odds with the Russian authorities on several occasions because it won't give encryption keys or cooperate with requests for data. As a result, the app was temporarily banned in Russia from 2018 until 2020. This restriction was later overturned following an unknown agreement reached by both parties. Durov has been known as a champion of digital freedom because to his defiance of political pressure, but he has also elevated Telegram to a central position in the privacy vs. public safety argument.

The arrest and its fallout have influenced Telegram's response to demands from international agencies. Although Durov is still refusing calls for backdoors or compromised encryption, the platform has made other efforts, such closing down extremist channels open to the public, to lessen illicit activity. Even in the face of mounting regulatory pressure, the company is committed to upholding user privacy because of Durov's worldview.

Actions Taken to Stop Illegal Behavior on the Platform

Due to its connections to criminal activities, including drug trafficking, cybercrime, and the recruitment of extremists, Telegram has been under intense investigation. As a result, the platform has adopted a number of measures to thwart unlawful activities while upholding its dedication to free speech and privacy. Content moderation in open channels and groups is one of Telegram's main strategies for resolving this problem. Teams employed by the corporation keep an eye on and shut down channels that are involved in illicit activity, like the selling of firearms or drugs, the exploitation of children, or the dissemination of extremist ideology.

Users on Telegram can also report questionable activities, and its moderation teams will analyze and investigate the reports. The platform's attempts to stop illicit behavior have been greatly aided by this reporting feature, since many illicit operations are reported by users who stumble across them in public or semi-public areas. Reported channels and groups that participate in illicit activities may be taken down, and the users who run them may face platform bans. But Telegram has a big problem with its secret channels and private chats, which are completely encrypted and unreadable by anyone on the company.

When it is appropriate, Telegram has collaborated with law enforcement to address illicit conduct in these encrypted places. The corporation has cooperated by supplying metadata in some circumstances, such as tracking when an account was active or its linked phone number, even if it does not disclose backdoor access or encryption keys. Several criminal networks that were utilizing Telegram for illicit reasons have been brought down as a result, but the platform's unwillingness to erode encryption limits its ability to assist with law enforcement.

Telegram has also stepped up measures to stop terrorism on the network in recent years. Telegram has collaborated more closely with agencies like Europol to detect and remove extremist content in response to demand from governments and watchdog groups. Telegram has tightened its efforts to prevent radical groups like ISIS, Al-Qaeda, and others from emerging under other names. These groups' channels have been taken down on a regular basis. Although radical groups still target the platform in an attempt to maintain their privacy, their efforts have decreased the amount of radical content that is visible on public channels.

In general, Telegram's approach to combating illicit activity has changed, placing more emphasis on content monitoring and working with law authorities. But its fundamental beliefs about user privacy and defiance of state coercion still shape its strategy, making it difficult to strike a balance between privacy and public safety.

Chapter 5: The Future of Messaging Apps

Changing Privacy Concerns and User Expectations

As technology advances, users' expectations for messaging apps also grow. In addition to rapid communication, users of today expect a platform that puts privacy, security, and user experience first. Users now demand different things from their messaging services due to growing awareness of data breaches, government surveillance, and corporate exploitation of personal information. Because of this, privacy issues have emerged as one of the main forces behind the creation and advancement of messaging services like WhatsApp, Signal, and Telegram.

Since protecting their conversations from outside parties has become a top priority for consumers, many messaging systems now come equipped with end-to-end encryption as standard. While encryption protects against unwanted access, it also raises questions about how criminals would abuse such privacy. Customers want to know that not only is their data safe, but also that the app provider has a clear policy for handling, storing, and potentially sharing user data. Users are scrutinizing privacy policies more than ever, and any vagueness or lack of openness might cause them to leave a platform.

Concurrently, there's a growing need for personal data control and customization. More choices regarding the duration of message storage, the method of erasing one's digital trail, and the degree of personal data required for registration are being requested by users. To give users more control over their communication, apps like Telegram have included features like secret chats and self-destructing messages.

Messaging applications have to stay ahead of regulatory developments as privacy rules become more stringent worldwide. The European Union's General Data Protection Regulation (GDPR) has upped the bar for privacy requirements, and other areas are starting to do the same. Businesses who break these laws could face severe penalties and lose the trust of their customers. The task for messaging apps in this changing climate will be to satisfy user privacy demands while negotiating ever-more complicated regulatory frameworks.

Balancing Safety and Freedom of Speech

A fundamental human right is the ability to express oneself, and messaging applications have been important in allowing people to do just that. However, messaging apps must balance free speech with security issues because they serve as forums for both public and private communication. This is especially challenging because these platforms are frequently used to disseminate hate speech, false information, and extreme beliefs.

Telegram and other messaging services have long portrayed themselves as bulwarks of free speech, providing users with a means of communication unhindered by government restrictions. For users in nations with authoritarian regimes, where governmental censorship is prevalent, this has proved especially crucial. But this dedication to free speech has also made these platforms vulnerable to misuse by those looking to disseminate damaging information, such as terrorist propaganda and hate speech.

Moving forward, messaging apps will have the problem of maintaining the principles of free expression while making sure their services are secure for all users. Numerous messaging applications have already implemented moderation procedures, which involve the removal of public channels or groups that disseminate offensive content. For example, Telegram has taken action to eliminate extremist information and channels linked with ISIS from its public channels, but it has come under fire for not doing more to stop illicit activity in private encrypted chats.

In the future, maintaining this equilibrium will become more challenging as authorities and lawmakers demand greater control over damaging content on these platforms. Overly strict regulation, however, has the potential to backfire by restricting free speech and driving users to less regulated, more decentralized platforms. In order to efficiently identify dangerous information without restricting valid free speech, messaging apps will need to create sophisticated moderation systems. This is a challenging task that calls for a delicate balancing act between technology, ethics, and legislation.

Suggestions for Communicating in a Changing Environment

A few factors will influence how people communicate in the upcoming years as we look to the future of messaging apps. The growing use of artificial intelligence (AI) in messaging platforms is one of the most noticeable changes. Though automated answers and chatbots powered by AI are currently widespread, future advancements will probably see AI play a bigger role in how people interact with messaging apps. AI might be used, for instance, to filter information, identify inappropriate behavior, and even improve user experience by providing more individualized communication tools.

Another trend that has the potential to change message is the emergence of decentralized platforms. Apps for communicating on blockchain, which offer even higher degrees of confidentiality and anonymity, are becoming more and more popular. These platforms provide consumers total autonomy over their communication and data, free from corporate interference or centralized authority. Although this is a positive development for privacy, it may also provide new difficulties for the authorities in controlling illicit content and ensuring user safety on these sites.

Future messaging is also anticipated to involve augmented reality (AR) and virtual reality (VR). Messaging apps may advance beyond text, audio, and video to incorporate immersive communication experiences that allow users to interact in 3D virtual locations as AR and VR technology becomes more widely used. This has the potential to completely transform both professional and personal communication by providing new avenues for connection outside of established communications formats.

Lastly, the future of communications may be shaped by the ongoing emergence of mega applications. Applications such as WeChat, which are available in China, have demonstrated how messaging can be included into a wider ecosystem that encompasses social networking, e-commerce, and payments. We may witness a future in which messaging applications function as primary centers for a variety of activities, making them indispensable tools for both personal and professional life, as other platforms, like WhatsApp, progress in this direction.

The future of messaging applications in this shifting environment will be determined by their capacity to manage the intricate interactions between technology, ethics, and regulation while striking a balance between privacy, security, and user pleasure. Our communication patterns for the foreseeable future will be shaped by platforms that can effectively adjust to these obstacles.

Conclusion

Thoughts on the Difficult Character of Communication

The idea of communication has always been complicated and dynamic, influenced by changes in societal conventions, technology, and human behavior. Thanks to messaging apps like Telegram, WhatsApp, and Signal, real-time, worldwide conversations are now more accessible than ever in the digital age, completely changing the way people communicate. Although these platforms have given people more power, they have also brought about a number of complications, mostly with relation to security, privacy, and freedom of speech.

In the digital age, communication is fundamentally different from information transmission. It entails negotiating a complex web of social, legal, and ethical issues. Originally designed to make quick and simple interactions possible, messaging applications are increasingly used for advocacy, business, and, regrettably, illegal activity. This dichotomy highlights the complex nature of communication in the modern world by acting as a vehicle for bad purpose as well as a tool for positive change.

One of the most important analyses of this complexity is the way in which features that give users power can also make bad actions possible. For example, end-to-end encryption, a feature intended to safeguard user privacy, has also made it easier for criminal activity to go undetected by law enforcement, such as drug trafficking, cybercrime, and terrorism. The conflict between security and abuse highlights the difficulties in maintaining communication systems in a way that safeguards law-abiding users while discouraging bad activity.

It's also challenging to implement a one-size-fits-all strategy because these platforms function in a variety of cultural, political, and legal contexts due to their global reach. The fact that what is deemed free speech in one nation may be viewed as hate speech in another, making these platforms' function as international communicators more challenging. Messaging applications have to balance these conflicting demands as they develop and work to create spaces where communication is still responsible, safe, and unrestricted.

The Way Ahead: Handling Security and Privacy in the Digital Age

The fine line between security and privacy will continue to be a major concern for messaging platforms as well as consumers as the digital era progresses. Security problems will only increase due to the growing reliance on messaging apps for personal, professional, and even financial transactions. Users are demanding more control and transparency as a result of growing awareness of how their personal data is handled, shared, and preserved.

For messaging apps, enhancing security features without sacrificing user privacy is one way to go forward. To guarantee that not even the platform provider can access user data, this may entail implementing zero-knowledge protocols and incorporating cutting-edge encryption techniques. But as security features get stronger, it will be harder to stop malicious actors from using these same technologies. More advanced content moderation techniques that can identify and stop bad activity without violating encryption or jeopardizing privacy are needed for messaging apps.

Adherence to regulations is an additional crucial element. Messaging platforms will need to adjust as governments around the world enact stronger data privacy legislation by making sure they both abide by the law and uphold their fundamental principles of protecting user privacy. Working with governments to combat illicit activity while protecting the privacy of legitimate users will be crucial to this effort.

Message apps must prioritize user education in addition to security and legal precautions. By improving the accessibility and clarity of privacy settings, individuals can regain more control over their digital presence. In addition to promoting responsible platform use, safer online environments can also be created by giving users the means to report questionable conduct.

Messaging applications need to find a way to balance user privacy, public safety, and technological advancement. Platforms that balance privacy and security will continue to prosper as a result of ongoing advancements in encryption, artificial intelligence, and decentralized technologies. These platforms will be able to navigate the intricacies of the digital age while upholding the confidence and security of its users.

www.ingramcontent.com/pod-product-compliance
Lightning Source LLC
Chambersburg PA
CBHW062124220526
45471CB00010B/3871